WELCOME WATER

The Sacrament of Baptism for
Parents, Sponsors, Children,
and Others

WELCOME WATER

*The Sacrament of Baptism for Parents,
Sponsors, Children,
and Others*

Welcome Water: The Sacrament of Baptism for Parents, Sponsors, Children, and Others

Contributors: *Steve Swanson, Heather Eeman Hammond*
Editors: *Barbara S. Wilson and Eileen K. Zahn*
Illustration and Design: *Circus Design*

Scripture quotations are from New Revised Standard Version Bible, copyright © 1989 Division of Christian Education of the National Council of the Church of Christ in the United States of America. Used by permission.

Materials identified as LBW are from Lutheran Book of Worship, copyright © 1978.

Materials identified as from the Small Catechism are from The Small Catechism by Martin Luther in Contemporary English, 1979 edition, copyright © 1960, 1968.

ISBN 0-8066-3699-8

Manufactured in U.S.A.
     0 1 2 3 4 5 6 7 8 9

INTRODUCTION

In the waters of Baptism we are reborn children of God.

LBW, p. 121

ou are planning a baptism—how wonderful! This book has been provided to help you prepare for baptism in the Christian church. Perhaps it is your own baptism, the culmination of years of yearning and searching. Perhaps it is your child who will be baptized, beginning a lifelong journey of faith.

Your pastor may simply hand this book to you, smile, and say, "Please read this." Or this book may be the starting point for conversation with your pastor or with others preparing for baptism about the significance of this once in a lifetime event.

Baptism matters to Christians because it mattered to Jesus and his early followers. Among the few specific instructions Jesus left his followers is "Go therefore and make disciples of all nations, baptizing them in the name of the Father and of the Son and of the Holy Spirit" (Matthew 28:19). Along with the command to baptize Jesus also gave a life-changing promise: "I am with you always" (Matthew 28:20).

When we are doused with God's welcome water in baptism, God immediately begins keeping that promise, and we are never the same. Forevermore the God we meet in Jesus will share every adventure, every disaster, and every joy that comes our way. Never will we be abandoned or forsaken.

Christians all over the world practice baptism as a sign of the new life that God gives us in Jesus and as a symbol of unity between all who bear the name Christian. Regardless of age, language, culture, gender, or background, the church welcomes all people to be washed in God's water of life.

Baptism is a sacrament. Sacraments have sometimes been described as God's "visible words," physical and tangible expressions of the mysterious presence of God's unconditional love in our common, ordinary lives. Just as the Christian faith believes that Jesus is God-made-flesh, we also understand sacraments to be God's Word-made-touchable.

Lutheran Christians have described sacraments as being the unity of God's "word, sign, and promise." That is why two sacraments—Holy Baptism and Holy Communion—have been recognized. Both:

+ relate to a biblical command ("Go...baptizing them in the name");
+ connect to God's word of promise ("I am with you always"); and
+ use earthly elements (water, bread, wine).

Please read *Welcome Water* with care. Mark things that surprise you or about which you have questions so you can discuss them with your pastor or other Christians.

The words printed in italics at the beginning of each section are taken from the baptismal service in *Lutheran Book of Worship* (LBW). Note these passages well and listen for them when you or your child receives God's welcome water!

THE WELCOME

We welcome you into the Lord's family.

We receive you as fellow members of the body of Christ,

children of the same heavenly Father,

and workers with us in the kingdom of God. LBW, p. 125

COME, MEET THE FAMILY

Baptism is a divine family welcome. First it is God's welcome, for in each baptism God wraps loving arms around a particular adult or child, teenager or baby, and says, "I choose you for my family. I adopt you as my very own. I put my sign and seal upon you. Forevermore you have a new name: Child of God."

Baptism is also a family welcome. Your local congregation is just one household in the whole family of God, its members just a few of the children of God, brothers and sisters eager to welcome the newest-born child of God into the family. The rest of God's family includes people of every time and place, people who lived long ago and people not yet born, all people who have turned or will turn to God in trust and hope.

Your congregation may have its own distinctive way of welcoming newly baptized persons, since customs vary from one place or culture to the next. For an analogy, consider how one workplace might welcome a new employee with treats at break time, while another workplace might play a practical joke on the newcomer! As varied as they are, both of these expressions of welcome celebrate arrival and presence. They offer relationship and acceptance. They anticipate a shared future. That's what the welcome of baptism is about too.

HUMAN AND DIVINE

Someone—a relative, a friend, a church member, or a pastor—may have encouraged you to take the step of seeking baptism. No person, however, can fully extend God's wondrously warm and gracious invitation. If the welcome you feel from your congregational family is not as warm as you wish, remember that God's whole and holy embrace is larger than any human expression. Even if the people you meet seem quiet, shy, or distant, God's invitation isn't weakened by such human frailties. Baptism is always God's clear and certain welcome into the Christian family.

REFLECTIONS

Jesus promised to be with you always. When was the last time you were consciously aware of God's presence? What difference did it make?

Recall a time when you were a newcomer. Who made you feel most welcome? What did that person do or say? What will you do when it is your turn to welcome a newcomer?

THE WONDER OF WATER

In the beginning your Spirit moved over the waters and you created

heaven and earth. By the gift of water you nourish and sustain us

and all living things. LBW, p. 122

DRIPPING WITH LIFE

Water may be our creator's most indispensable invention. We can't live without it. Before birth we live in water; it protects us until we are ready for air. From then on, we must drink daily or we will die. One can go many days, or even weeks, without food, but not water. Water sustains human life, as well as the plants and animals humans rely upon for food, shelter, and clothing. Astronomers scan distant planets for evidence of old riverbeds or dry lake beds, or even the telltale marks of erosion. Any of those signs would signal that water had once been present, and water means life could have existed on that planet. Evidence of water is evidence of life.

For Christians water becomes the substance of which miracles are made. Jesus Christ submerged one miracle in another. He mixed water with some sublimely important words to create a new thing. The result is baptism, a liquid sign of life and hope. But water also symbolizes two other important truths about baptism.

INTO THE DEPTHS

In Holy Baptism our gracious heavenly Father liberates us from sin and death by joining us to the death and resurrection of our Lord Jesus Christ (LBW, p. 121).

Although water allows life to grow and flourish, water can also drown and destroy. The water of baptism symbolizes drowning the power of evil that keeps a person estranged from God. Making a few spiritual improvements isn't enough to overcome human beings' fatal attraction to that which is foul and flawed. We must be rebirthed by God in order to become children of God. A gush of water signals the beginning of spiritual rebirth, just as it does a physical birth.

King David longed for just such a cleansing. He may have been Israel's greatest ruler, but he was also a seriously flawed human being. His overwhelming desire to possess the wife of another man resulted in the death and destruction of innocent people. When David finally faced up to what he had done he was overcome with grief and guilt. In despair he cried out to God, "Wash me thoroughly…cleanse me from my sin." (Psalm 51:2). In the Christian church God lifts such unbearable shame and guilt through the death and resurrection of Jesus, an experience we are invited to make our own by means of an unusual bath.

A PUBLIC BATH

In many cultures bathing is usually a public event. People gather at the river or the public bathhouse. The joy of cleanliness and the enjoyment of community go together. Baptism is like that. Cleansing from sin takes place in the midst of the church family, among the people who stand ready to welcome the newborn

Christian with joy. In the family of God, joy shared is joy multiplied.

Occasionally baptisms take place in hospitals during emergencies. Chaplains, nurses, and midwives do them. Years ago "private" baptisms (with only the immediate family and sponsors in attendance) were more common. Several factors, including infant mortality, contagious disease, and the difficulty of travel contributed to the practice. Today the church strongly urges people to schedule baptisms during a regular worship service so the gathered brothers and sisters have an opportunity to offer their public welcome and commitment to the newest child of God in their midst.

REFLECTIONS

Think about your usual household routines. How many different ways do you use water? How might some of those uses of water serve as symbols of baptism's benefits?

THE SUBSTANCE OF LIFE

By water and the Holy Spirit

we are made members of the Church

which is the body of Christ.

As we live with him and with his people,

we grow in faith, love, and obedience to the will of God.

LBW, p. 121

REAL THINGS

Christians believe God is the most real thing in the universe. In fact, our reality exists only because God sustains time and space in such a way that our existence is possible. Within the world as we know it, God's work makes God known to us. Indeed, one of the most astonishing claims of Christian faith is that God earnestly desires to be known, by all of us. "No longer shall they teach one another, or say to each other, 'Know the Lord,' for they shall all know me, from the least of them to the greatest, says the Lord; for I will forgive their iniquity, and remember their sin no more" (Jeremiah 31:34).

God engages us in several ways. We meet God the creator in the intricate grandeur and profound stillness of the universe. God the Savior enters our existence in Jesus who, being fully human and fully God, revealed in his earthly life all that can be humanly known of God. God the Holy Spirit accompanies believers moment by moment, actively guiding, encouraging, and strengthening the children of God.

God also engages us through the ancient words of the Bible. The Spirit works to make the scriptures bear to us the living Word of God, Jesus. Viewed simply as a book, the Bible is a diverse collection of stories, histories, poetry, advice, and ideas, as recalled by people who reported life-changing encounters with God in times past. But when those old words come alive for us with depth and a powerful shock of understanding, Christians recognize the working of God, making the splendor of the Creator and the counsel of the Spirit active in human hearts and minds by leading us to an encounter with the living Word, Jesus Christ.

Similarly, God arranges for us to meet Jesus in Holy Baptism and Holy Communion. In these sacraments the living Word of God is combined with things we touch and taste. Both sacraments incorporate things upon which physical life depends: food and water. The food, the bread and wine of Holy Communion, we leave for another book. For Christians, water is where real life begins to be known.

AN INVITATION TO LIFE

We give you thanks for freeing your sons and daughters from the power of sin and for raising them up to a new life through this holy sacrament (LBW, p. 124).

People may begin to respond to God's welcoming invitation at any stage of life. Since ancient times the Christian church has baptized both infants and adults. In fact the church treats infants as if they were adults, and adults as if they were infants when it comes to baptism.

We baptize infants as if they were adults, welcoming them with words much too large for them, and promises their parents, sponsors, and congregation must help them appreciate as they grow in years. But then we baptize adults as if they were helpless infants, bathing them and clothing them with God's love in Christ, an act no one is able to accomplish for themselves, by themselves. Baptism belongs to people of any age or stage in life.

Some Christians believe baptism should follow the achievement of certain standards of spiritual growth and formation. In contemporary culture, many people think children ought to be free to choose their own religion, rather than having adults make that decision for them. Lutheran Christians say, "Wait a minute! Who is doing the choosing here?" Lutherans emphasize that baptism reflects God's irrevocable choice to love the one being baptized, whether or not that love is ever returned. Baptism is not about choosing a god, but about God choosing us. Through Christian education and faith formation, adults, as well as children, learn to respond more and more deeply to the love God has so freely poured out on them in baptism.

THE TIME IS NOW

An infant flourishes in the care of loving parents without the slightest understanding of the commitment and sacrifice required to provide that care. In the same way the blessings of baptism come to those who are baptized with or without their understanding of what is happening.

Baptism is a wonder that may be better sensed than understood. Imagine a spectacular sunset, dazzling the western sky with power and beauty. That sunset might be understood in formulas representing the wavelengths of visible light or calculated in terms of the orbital position of the sun. That knowledge might help you comprehend the sunset, but it won't help you glory in it, which is, after all, the proper use of a wondrous sunset! Neither adults nor children can fully comprehend the gift of God's love in baptism. All we can do is glory in God's love, seeking to understand as we are able. Baptism is not about whether we feel ready to understand God, but about trusting that God already understands us.

So when should you or your child or your baby be baptized? Sooner, rather than later! As an adult or youth, you are ready as soon as you realize you long to be a child of God. For an infant, plan the baptism as soon as he or she is able to be with the larger family in church. Many healthy newborns attend worship their first Sunday home from the hospital!

REFLECTIONS

What difference is there in the way you think about God and the way you feel about God?

What difference does it make if you choose God, or if God chooses you? Who is more likely to have a change of heart?

THE THREE PROMISES

Child of God, you have been sealed by the Holy Spirit and marked

with the cross of Christ forever. LBW, *p.* 124

Lutherans baptize with three generous scoops of water, poured out in the name of the Father, and of the Son, and of the Holy Spirit. In some congregations the person being baptized simply stands at or is held over the baptismal font as the water is poured. In other congregations, baptismal candidates enter a pool of water where still more water is poured over their heads. Either form is a real baptism, so long as it is done in the name of the triune God.

The pastor places both hands on the head of the newly baptized and prays for the Holy Spirit to come with wisdom, understanding, counsel, might, knowledge, fear (awe) of the Lord, and joy. Then the pastor's fingers trace the sign of the cross on the forehead of the baptized, sometimes using fragrant oil for this anointing. After one three-year-old's baptism the child made a point of telling everyone who came to the reception, "Pastor put a cross on my head, and she said it's going to be there forever!" That child had it right! The mark of the cross is an indelible mark, a sign that one is now and forever a child of God. As children, therefore, baptized Christians may expect to share in the riches of God's household.

God secures that hope with three powerful promises. These promises are just as necessary, just as true, for an infant as for an octogenarian. Since 1529 when Luther wrote the Small Catechism, Lutheran Christians have put it this way (italics added): "In Baptism God *forgives sin, delivers from death and devil*, and *gives everlasting salvation* to all who believe what he has promised" (The Small Catechism, p. 23).

PROMISE 1: FORGIVENESS OF SINS

Most adults will readily acknowledge, at least in private, that they have sinned. But a baby? What possible offense can a newborn have committed? Common sense tells us that a baby hasn't done anything—yet! The claim that people are sinners from birth is impossible to understand or accept if sin is understood simply as something a person does. Christians see sin as something far more insidious: a fatal flaw in our being, not just in our doing. To be "in sin" means to be separated from God and, as a result, to behave badly toward those with whom we share the planet. The proof is in this: even though God is the source of life, we have no inkling of God as we begin to live it. If we come to know God later in life it is only because we were introduced by people who themselves were once introduced to God by others. Since sin severed our intimate connection with God, we are peevish, contrary, and selfish from the moment of birth.

Think about it. When a baby is hungry or needs a fresh diaper does she or he think, "Well, I know how tired the folks are these days, so I'll hold back for an hour or so and let them rest"? Of course not. That baby is totally absorbed in the immediacy of his or her own wants and needs, and can't begin to consider anyone else's well-being. That's how babies naturally are. That's what it is to be naturally sinful: ignorant of God, careless of others.

What is more, our relentless self-absorption doesn't ever naturally disappear. Adults become more sophisticated in voicing their demands, but it still comes down to "I want what I want when I want it!" We didn't choose to be that way; it's how we're born. So it is fitting to baptize babies.

Of course babies don't instantly become unselfish the moment they are baptized. Neither do children, teenagers, or adults. But they are marked by God as persons being drawn toward God-likeness. We become God's children growing toward spiritual strength and maturity. We begin learning to cultivate the fruits of the Spirit: "love, joy, peace, patience, kindness, generosity, faithfulness, gentleness, and self-control" (Galatians 5:22-23).

Those fruitful qualities describe the sort of human being Christians long to become: Christ-like persons, secure in their identity as children of God. Growing toward God-likeness begins with God's initiative, expressed in the divine promise of baptism. "Living in the covenant of their Baptism and in communion with the Church, they may lead godly lives until the day of Jesus Christ" (*LBW*, p. 122).

PROMISE 2: DELIVERANCE FROM DEATH AND THE DEVIL

Baptism delivers us despite death and the devil. The moment we are born, death becomes inevitable. God reminds us that we need fear neither birth and growth, nor aging and death. "Neither death, nor life...nor anything else in all creation, will be able to separate us from the love of God in Christ Jesus our Lord" (Romans 8:38-39).

Baptism does not deliver us from death, but through it. Death becomes the next-to-last stop on our life's journey, not the end of the line. We need not fear death because in baptism we are sealed by the Holy Spirit, marked with the cross of Christ, and wrapped in the arms of God forever. We are ushered through and beyond death.

In a sense, the baptized person has already practiced dying, through Christ, as well as rehearsed rising up to new life. The power of death, which we experience as a terror of the unknown, is broken. We've been there. We've done that. Death is highly overrated in comparison with the life God gives!

The power of evil that Martin Luther's Catechism calls "the devil" is closely related to the power of death. The devil deals in deception and death in all its forms (John 8:44). The concept of death embodies not only the cessation of bodily functions, but also every wound to mind, body, and spirit that diminishes the fullness of life and pushes people toward despair.

Evil is a fact of life. The devil hopes it will drive us to despair, for despair is as fatal to the heart and mind as poison is to the body. Evil needn't bother about the body if it can kill the spirit first. When Christians pray "Deliver us from evil," it doesn't mean they expect to be excused from enduring the hurts of life. It means they look to God to rescue them from despair. In baptism God promises deliverance, despite death and the devil, not without death and the devil. Since through baptism we have practiced dying well, we are ready to be raised up, at any time, to life without end.

PROMISE 3: EVERLASTING SALVATION

Life, more life than we ever thought possible, is the purpose of baptism. Through Jesus Christ God has succeeded in overcoming the terrible trio of sin, death, and the devil, the obstacles that prevent people from living in intimate, joyous relationship with God and all God's children. Christ has triumphed! Life is yours for the living!

Reflections

How do you react to the statement "sin is a fatal flaw in our being, not in our doing"? Is it easier or more difficult to think of sin as specific violations of well-defined rules?

If you were certain that you would live forever, how might it change the way you live today?

SALVATION:
WHAT ON EARTH
IS IT FOR?

By the baptism of his own death and resurrection

your beloved Son has set us free from the bondage to sin and death,

and has opened the way to the joy and freedom of everlasting life.

LBW, p. 122

THE FUTURE IS NOW

We are not only saved from sin, death, and the power of the devil, we are saved for an abundant, everlasting life that begins here and now, and will be fulfilled in eternity. Through baptism we gain a sacred identity as a child of God. The world is quick to label people: winner, loser, prom queen, geek. In a world that often treats us like nobodies, baptism insists we are somebodies, priceless children of God and heirs of eternity. In the power of our baptism we declare, "I may not look like much yet, but just you wait!"

GOD ISN'T FINISHED YET

Even though the persons we shall be may not be obvious to the world, baptism means we have already started to become the people God longs for us to be. We are not yet pure, that is, totally devoted to God, but being baptized means we can drown the devious thoughts and deeds of yesterday and, by the grace of God, begin again today as a free, renewed self. The Small Catechism says that baptism "means that our sinful self, with all its evil deeds and desires, should be drowned through daily repentance; and that day after day a new self should arise to live with God in righteousness and purity forever" (p. 25).

Baptism frees us from bondage to sin, from our own sins as well as from the lingering effects of sins others have committed against us. Daily repentance and renewal is the antidote to guilt and shame over what we have done, and an effective treatment for our bitterness and resentment over what others have done to us.

ONCE AND FOREVER

Anyone baptized in any Christian church, of any denomination, in any language, in any part in the world, is considered baptized forever by Lutherans and most other Christians. We never rebaptize. Baptism is first and foremost God's personal word, God's choice, God's promise. Since God keeps every promise, there is no need for God to promise again and again, as though God's intentions were uncertain. One baptism lasts a lifetime, even if someone wanders from his or her holy inheritance and drops out of the community of faith for awhile. God's eternal promise means that God will seek out the lost, continually working through persons and situations to call the wanderer back. When the wanderer returns, joy abounds in heaven and on earth! The individual may wish to reaffirm his or her baptism, but there is no need for God to recommit to the individual through another baptism.

AFFIRMATION OF BAPTISM

Do you intend to continue in the covenant God made with you in Holy Baptism? (*LBW*, p. 201).

While Christians do well to remember and reclaim their baptismal identity on a daily basis, a formal affirmation can be especially valuable at life's turning points. Becoming a parent or grandparent, beginning a marriage or ending a relationship, starting a new job or retiring, the children of God may use the rite of Affirmation of Baptism (*LBW*, p. 198) at any significant passage in life. In congregational worship it is most commonly done in three ways:

✦ At Confirmation those who have completed a significant time of instruction signal their readiness to assume greater responsibility in the life of the church by Affirmation of Baptism.

✦ When Christians baptized in other denominations join a Lutheran congregation they may be received by Affirmation of Baptism.

✦ People who departed from their faith and have returned may be restored to membership in the church by Affirmation of Baptism.

WHEN THE MOMENT COMES

Chances are you have observed baptisms with more interest as you prepare for this one. Soon it will be your turn. Prayers will be offered. Water, warm and abundant, will be splashed. The sign of the cross will be made on the forehead. A candle may be lighted. Suddenly you, or your loved one, will belong.

You may experience a sense of deep joy and serenity. The moment may seem larger than life, but not because there is anything magical about the water or the pastor. It's just plain water. The pastor is no more (and no less) a holy being than you are, just a child of God called to the work of presiding at the congregation's celebration of Word and Sacrament. Stripped of the ceremony, baptism is simply earth's water and God's Word, fused by the Holy Spirit in the midst of the family of God.

REFLECTIONS

Suppose someone asked, "Now that you've done this baptism thing, what does that make you?" What might you say?

Name-calling hurts, no matter what our age. How might you help a child claim her baptismal identity as a way of coping with cruel remarks?

Think of an embarrassing episode you would like to put behind you. How can your baptism help you hold your head up again?

ESPECIALLY FOR PARENTS

O God, giver of all life, look with kindness

upon the fathers and mothers of these children.

Let them ever rejoice in the gift you have given them.

Make them teachers and examples of righteousness for their children.

Strengthen them in their own Baptism

so they may share eternally with their children

the salvation you have given them, through Jesus Christ our Lord.

LBW, p. 124

IT'S TIME TO GROW

As you prepare for the baptism of the remarkable child God has entrusted to your care, consider your own spiritual life. Entering into a baptismal covenant on behalf of your child creates a perfect opportunity for you to grow in your own relationship with God. Children notice what their parents value. If the life of faith matters to you, it will matter to your child. Tending to your own spiritual growth provides your child with a valuable model, and will very likely make you a more effective and loving parent as well.

In the baptism ceremony you will promise to nurture the spiritual growth of your child in specific ways, to: "faithfully bring them to the services of God's house, and teach them the Lord's Prayer, the Creed, and the Ten Commandments...place in their hands the Holy Scriptures and provide for their instruction in the Christian faith" (*LBW*, p. 121).

The splash of baptism water happens just once, but it marks the beginning of lifelong spiritual growth and learning. Your child is a spiritual being who needs to connect to God. She has an emerging self-understanding as a created being, especially designed by, loved by, sought after, and saved by God.

As you nurture your child's physical, emotional, and social growth, attend to spiritual development as well. Pray for your child. Pray with your child. Seek help from God and from your congregation too. During the earliest months and years, a child survives by trusting in you and other loving caregivers. If you have proven trustworthy, this comfortable trust will in time extend naturally to God. Your child's faith will grow through a whole range of formative experiences blessed by the awesome workings of the Spirit.

THE BAPTISM DAY

On the day of the baptism, you and the sponsors will stand together with the pastor at the font. You will be asked if you promise to oversee the faith formation of your child, and you will respond, "I do." A little later in the service you and the sponsors will be asked for another pledge: "Do you renounce all the forces of evil, the devil, and all his empty promises?" (*LBW*, p. 123). The church is asking you and, by extension, your child to choose sides in the battle of good and evil. You and the sponsors you have chosen answer, "I do."

Next comes the Apostles' Creed. This is the church's most ancient summary of what it understands to be true about God the Father, God the Son, and God the Holy Spirit. It is told in the form of the story of what God has done in this world, and what Christians believe God is about to do in the world to come. Each of the three parts of the creed will be introduced with a question: Do you believe in God the Father? Do you believe in Jesus Christ, the Son of God? Do you believe in God the Holy Spirit? The congregation will join you in answering each question aloud using the words of the Apostles' Creed.

The promises you and the sponsors make on behalf of your child create a bond between you, a lifetime partnership of loving concern for your child. The responsibility is great, but you can rely on your congregation to support you prayerfully and practically in this child's faith formation.

REFLECTIONS

What helped you choose sponsors? What expectations do you have for their role in raising this child?

How do you understand your child's baptism as an affirmation of your own? In what ways has it already pushed you into reexamining your faith?

ESPECIALLY FOR SPONSORS OF YOUNG CHILDREN

I present _____*name*_____ *to receive*

the Sacrament of Holy Baptism. LBW, *p. 121*

UNIQUE ROLE

You have been asked to be a sponsor for a child who is about to be baptized in the Christian church. What does that mean?

No doubt you feel honored to have been chosen. But being chosen to be a sponsor is much more than a nice gesture. Long ago when Christian parents often didn't live to see their children reach adulthood, parents chose sponsors or "godparents" who would, if it became necessary, take the children into their home and raise them in Christian faith. Although today the role of baptismal sponsor is entirely distinct from the role of legal guardian, your commitment to this child is still critically important. You have been asked to be an adult friend and mentor, encouraging this child to grow in relationship with Jesus Christ.

How will you fulfill your responsibilities? To begin, add that child to your daily prayer list! Then begin to prepare for the baptism day. You may want to reread pages 121-125 of *Lutheran Book of Worship* with your new role in mind. Notice that you promise to support both the child and the parents. Notice the words you will speak to affirm the grounding of faith you will strive to pass on to this child. The congregational welcome spoken at the conclusion of the ceremony highlights the fact that the Sacrament of Baptism is the moment of welcome into God's family, a family in which you will serve as the closest of relatives.

A LIFELONG COMMITMENT

Over the years you will have many opportunities to fulfill the promises you make at the baptism. Mark the anniversary of the baptism on your calendar along with other important occasions. Send a card each year to remind the child of the day he or she became God's child. Books and toys which tell God's story can be appropriate gifts to honor the child's baptismal birthday.

As the child grows, stay connected. If you are close by, make a point to attend church-related functions with the family. If you cannot see each other often, be deliberate about phone calls and notes. Try to be the child's spiritual mentor and expect to mature in your own faith through this relationship.

Nothing your friends or family ever ask of you will be more important than sponsoring their child. Take the assignment seriously. Join the parents in guiding this child to grow up as a person of faith and integrity.

REFLECTIONS

How did you feel when you were asked to be a sponsor? What are the three most important actions you will take to support this child and his or her family?

What will you do in the next three years to grow closer to God?

ESPECIALLY FOR SPONSORS OF ADULTS AND YOUTH

I present _____name_____ *to receive*

the Sacrament of Holy Baptism. LBW, p. 121

HONOR AND RESPONSIBILITY

You have been honored with an invitation to become a baptismal sponsor for someone who is longing to be baptized in the Christian church. For the next few years, perhaps longer, you are going to be a mentor in the spiritual growth of this person. You will become companions on the journey of faith.

Initially your responsibility is to guide and accompany the candidate through the process of instruction and baptism. Begin by adding that person to your daily prayer list. Prepare yourself for the baptism by reviewing pages 121-125 in *Lutheran Book of Worship* with your new role in mind.

Soon your role shifts to one of helping the baptized establish wholesome habits of faith:

- daily prayer;
- weekly worship;
- participation in discipleship and learning opportunities; and
- active service in the congregation and/or community.

If you and the baptized are members of the same congregation it may be easier for you to help the baptized person make friends and feel at home in his or her new family. If you worship in different communities, you can still encourage the baptized to try out different activities and groups. While the congregation speaks a warm welcome to the newly baptized at the conclusion of the baptismal rite, individual members may be shy about reaching out to their new brother or sister in faith. Don't hesitate to call the pastor to discuss plans for assimilating the newly baptized into the life of the congregation. Like young seedlings, new Christians must have consistent support and nurture if they are to grow deeply and fruitfully in faith. Look for ways to stay connected with the person you are sponsoring. Phone calls, cards, and remembrances on the anniversary of the baptism are additional ways you can support the baptized even if you can't spend much time together.

In your sponsoring relationship you will probably start out as the teacher. Try never to lecture, but always to initiate conversations that invite the baptized to reflect on faith matters, and so to discover God working in him or her and through him or her. For example, ask to hear the whole story of how the newly baptized person came to faith in Jesus Christ. Note how persons and events combined to lead your friend to faith, and call attention to the fact that God was working with loving purpose in his or her life long before your friend even realized God cared.

While you may start out as the identified mentor, expect also to be a learner. The person you sponsor will likely have questions that will challenge you and insights that will amaze you. Seek understanding together, and affirm the wondrous growth happening before your eyes. Remember, as Paul wisely noted in 1 Corinthians 3:7, there is "one who plants...one who waters...but [it is] only God who gives the growth."

REFLECTIONS

Think of 24 ways to express your care for the person you are sponsoring. Schedule at least two each month for the next year. Here are some ideas:

1. Loan or give a "how to pray" book.

2. Attend a concert of Christian music together.

3. Send a card (or flowers) on the baptismal anniversary.

4. Attend Lenten worship together.

5. Send an interesting clipping.

6. Send an encouraging e-mail.

7.

8.

9.

10.

11.

12.

13.

14.

15.

16.

17.

18.

19.

20.

21.

22.

23.

24.

ESPECIALLY FOR CHILDREN

By water and the Holy Spirit

we are made members of the Church. LBW, p. 121

aptism is about water—a great splash of water.

We need water to live and grow. We need water to feel good and clean. If you have looked at a globe, you'll remember how much of it is blue. That's where the water is! All of that blue! Raindrops and oceans, a cup to drink and tears in our eyes all show us what an important part of God's creation water is.

God even uses water to show us how very much we are loved. In baptism a pastor uses three scoops of plain water, along with the promises God has made in the Bible. Through the water and the words, God says, "Welcome! You are now my beloved child!" The water in baptism is welcome water!

Soon you, or someone in your family, will be baptized. Baptism is God's loving way of showing us that we are special, and promising that we have a place in God's family forever. You probably already know many people who are baptized. They are part of God's family too.

When a girl or a boy or a man or a woman is baptized, everyone in the congregation hears the person's name and promises to help the person live as a child of God.

Use your finger to draw a cross shape on your forehead. There! That's just what the pastor will do after splashing some water on the head of the baptized person. The sign of the cross is invisible, but it lasts forever. It means the baptized person is a child of God always. Any time you want to remind yourself of how much God loves you, draw that cross on your forehead. When you do it, think of God putting great, loving arms around you, holding you until you feel happy and safe, then setting you down gently, and watching over you while you run and play some more. You are baptized. God will be there for you forever.

REFLECTIONS

Draw a picture about baptism.